Got to Keep it Moving

SE SCOTT

Thoughts to Think About

The point is this: **WE MOVE**! *And we must keep moving, hopefully with purpose and vision, until we accomplish what we set out to achieve.*

Movement *is a blessing from God. Remember, He was pretty busy Himself creating the world in six days. His actions during that time can be an example to and for us in our time. Have a set of goals and keep plugging away at them until all are done. Then REST on the seventh day, just like our Father.*

"Got to Keep It Moving" is similar to that unshakable stance that our Father took during the creation. It is an unshakable and determined stance that does not make excuses. Carry On!
This second book of poetry has a perspective that is faith driven and solution orientated; these poems are also about obstacles, love, pain, and how we see ourselves. In the mist of these things, we have got to keep it moving'! We got to believe that God is on our side, inside of us helping us be who He called us to be. Life continuously throws curve balls, but we got to keep it moving. Carry on! That is the kind of persistence it takes to live courageously.

SE Scott

CONTENTS

Thoughts to Think About

1. Challenges

2. I. D.

3. A Rock and a Hard Place

How to Beat Up a Friend
That Place Called Home
Sometimes
Someone Cares for You
Wounded-hearted Warriors
Your Heart is in His Hands
Joy to Come
Stop!

4. Got Faith

Where Faith Lives
Say What He Said
Not This Time
Got to Keep It Moving
You Got to Go
Struck Some Gold

5. And Love

Out on a Limb
Family Drama
When You Come Back to Me
Following Destiny
Just Do It
Benefits
Love is Going Crazy
No Lack of Love in Him
Charity

6. Now & Forever

Fired Up
Dreams
Habitations

A Holy Nazarene
Jesus Christ, the Holy One
Forever

Acknowledgements

About the Author

CHALLENGES

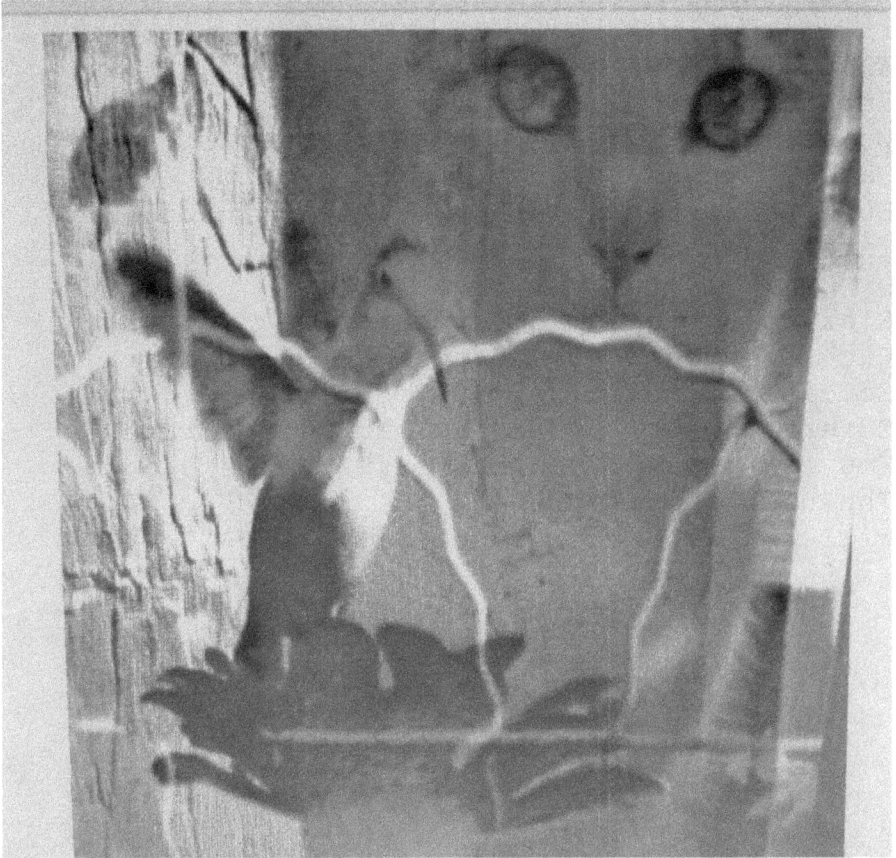

Push Past

Burden or blessing, you decide
The world has changed from the great divide
You got older, but didn't see
Multi-colored people in your destiny

What will you leave?
For young minds to ponder
Do you care if generations wander?
Gangs, drugs, an underworld of crime
Push past rhetoric that separates
Time to grab hands, communicate, relate

Risk what you would never do
Each one teach one or two
Education, politics, business or health
Entertainment, media, spread the wealth
You can't take it with you; so take heed
The next group coming
Will you help them succeed?

Yesterday's Self

Full of bluff
A whole lot of stuff, a no go destination
Procrastination
but you are more than enough
That is what I am told

Keep moving forward, be bold
Unleash those gifts put on hold
Love! Learn how to let go
Keep it moving, no matter what
You may think or know
Speak your words loud, be clear
Be the star of your show!

Have the courage to crush doubt
Just be beautiful inside and out

Small Adjustments

There is nothing wrong with thinking BIG
It is the thing to do
Embrace the dreams inside your heart
Until they all come true

Do not neglect small adjustments
Do them along the way
Attitude means a lot
Manners can save the day

Look beyond the box you are in
Look beyond yourself
Give a smile; lend a hand
Reach out help someone else

Small adjustments do more
than "the big thing" you search for
A little faith is all you need
to break down any door
Small adjustments pave the way
to dreams and so much more

Snow Top

Sometimes
I want to get back to where I left off
My best effort does not succeed
Ha, ha time laughs then accelerates in speed

Need to be more like Snow Top who
Gets up early
Ready in mind
An early bird, focused, refined
His predawn movements
That's the way
Snow Top rarely strays from

Keep Learning the Way

How to get through; how to tap in
To your potential hidden within
Valuable gems submerged in time, but not mined
Exchanged for something costing a dime
This is how it goes for a time

If one small drop ever seeps
If one imagined truth ever creeps
Into your heart of impeachable times
Destiny would be caught
Pirates would be caged
Revelation would come, setting the gauge
Stronger, higher eruptions, quakes

We are not here by mistake

It lingers long, that thing inside
Will you wake up?
Get moving, abide
Focused energy with no delay
Consequences diminish
As you learn the Way
Use half the time; there is hope.
Be gone, bright star! Elope!

Growing Taller

Grow taller, and smarter
Leave smaller behind

As you grow, you will see
Your precious talents, a destiny
Leave smaller behind

From the inside to the outside
Share your gifts with the world
Be a doctor, or singer
Be a writer; you choose
Study harder and get smarter
That is the way to never lose

You are special
You are gifted,
Leave smaller behind

I applaud you
I support you
And I love you being great

Keep on going until you make
Your purpose, dear precious, your fate
Grow taller, and smarter
Leave smaller behind

Give your talent, live your dream
Be that person others scream for
From the inside to the outside

There's no one else like you!

Operation Mustard Seed

All I needed was to lose a few
Nothing major but a challenge to do
I tried and tried, but the sweets and cake
Made it hard for weight to vacate
The premises grew large, overlapped
On top of that I would take a nap
What's a girl to do?

"How much do you weigh?" Others asked
Denying the evidence, I simply walked away
This happened during the guerilla years
I longed for a strategy, an answer for jeers.

The answer came when a mustard seed
Settled in my head
"Walk with a walker in early morn"
That challenge sprouted; the task was on!

Let me tell you that first day
How my body squeaked
Wanted badly to walk away, but that seed said,
"Stay"!
And I was no punk; a coward I could not be
This fight was going down
A war rose in me!

Dreams can come true with exerted sweat
Plant seeds in abundance; toss out your nets
Evacuate! Evacuate! New territories found!
Inches will soon vanish, then see pounds
Drop like butter, like a bay of pigs
Jump into the sea!

Victory Lives Today

You told me to walk on water
Light shining through
I stepped out like Peter
It was the thing to do
Challenge comes with triumph
Risk is just the best
Awesome is experience
Sail high above the tests

If I stay in focus
Maybe I will succeed
Those blatant distractions
In my eyes do breed

When I looked around
Noticed my affairs
I conferred with Panic
While still standing there
There on that water
Fear began to beg
"Pay attention, please"
All in my head
"What's the matter with you?
Leave a girl alone!"
This is how it happens
Basking in the zone
On the water front
Next--I don't know
Will I sink or swim
Hold that anchor fixed on Him

Alpha and Omega
Promised never to stray
True to His word
Victory lives today!

You Bad, Sister Girl

To Vanessa

I will not Bogart you
Just wanted you to see
Our last conversation was the epitome
Of intellectual pleasure
A meeting of the minds
So hard today another
Sister friend to find
To talk and talk a heap
To laugh about the world
Explore the old and new
With a bad sister girl
Those hours were full of power
Those husbands fell asleep
We could not let go
Conversation rich, and deep

And thanks,
You bought my book
Keep Smiling, Standing Strong
On Amazon not Nook
For bad sister girls

Your Wealthy Place

Do not say you have no control
It gives the enemy an edge, a foothold
A glimpse into your destiny
A chance to heist the best you can be

Told you before God's at the helm
Got to move over to the faith realm
Not only does He guide, He keeps eyes
On all that concerns you

To believe otherwise is not the thing to do
Walk in your wealthy place
Deception—that's the enemy's game
Remember, there is power in Jesus' name

His life, His works
Read the Bible and review
The mind of Christ lives within you
Walk in your wealthy place

I. D.

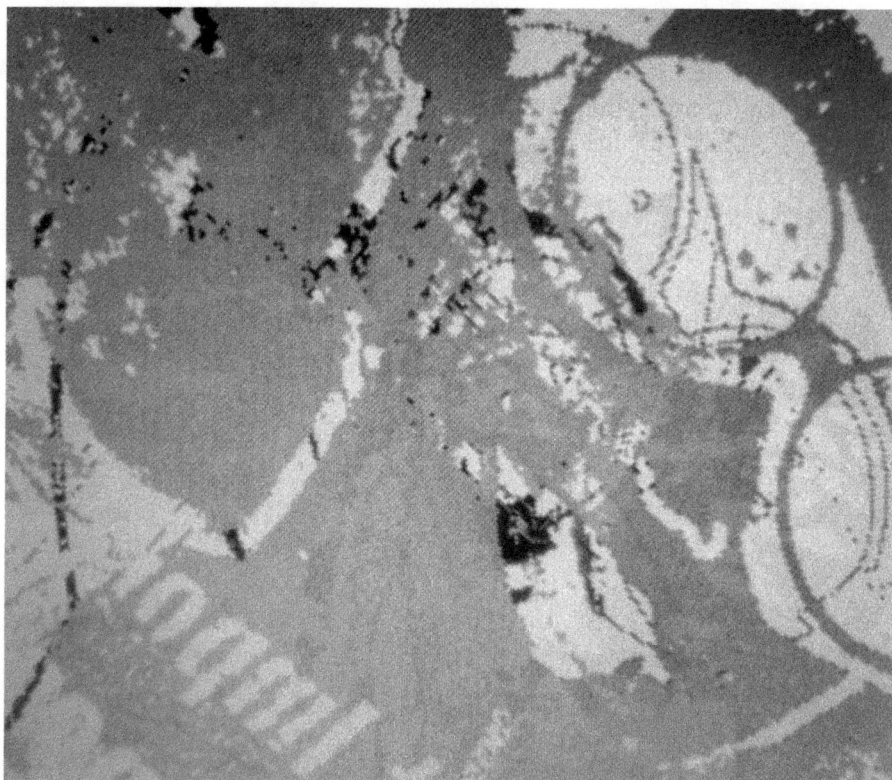

You Are Beautiful, Wonderfully Made

I am a woman dark at that
On the outside
Inside intact
I love all that is me

In a world that chooses to see
Stereotyped perspectives
And every degree
Of given nature, pedigree
Shaping thoughts
How others should be

Stay on guard because it is hard
To teach children well
Do not let things pass, giving in
to the great harass, a bombardment of thought
Oppressing others
Like it ought to be that way

No! Stay on guard
A tender heart can take a stand
for whatever
Just command it to be so
Always fight for what is right
It helps with sleep throughout the night

I am a woman dark at that
Would not matter if blue or black
God's hand is in this plan
He has for me in this land

"You are beautiful wonderfully made!"
Like hearing that; love being a shade
His word is truth; that is fact
He made me beautiful! He made me black!

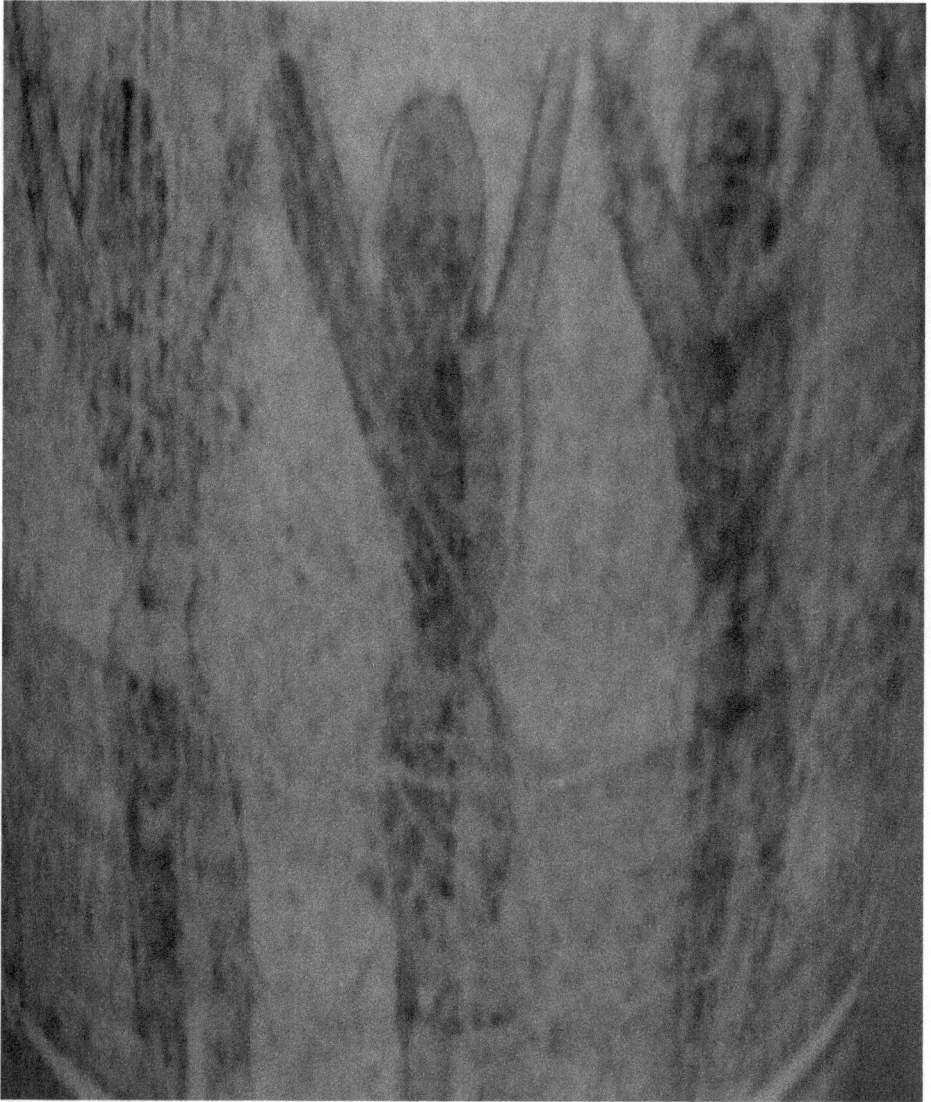

What Nobody Thought

God gives us value, not the world
We are precious just like pearls
He can make us whatever He chooses
In His presence, nobody ever loses

Our guiding light, our bird in the hand
Regardless of strife, it is His plan
That lifts us above the carnal clan
When it happens "they" won't understand
The life they see is a testimony

Because only He can make us what nobody
thought
Stunned, amazed and they ought
To join our worship that brought--victory
Out of that place they expected us to be

Surprises! He's full of them! Isn't He?

This World of Gullibility

There is more to life; you see, than living in
a fantasy
Whatever distraction it is; your total self
you give
A sacrificial lamb, negating the great I am
Somewhere deep inside

Brother, too, did hide
What God put in his heart
Talents, gifts and art
To be a better man
Not lost in anywhere land,
But lofty goals pursue
Take hold of courage in lieu
Of hours times hours a day
Descending distraction's way
A dismal life of decay

Barriers can lock out
Distractions, fears, and doubt
Enemies, laden in you
Press their ilk forcefully through
Amusing similar friends

Turn your strong spirit away
You are not destined to stay in this world of
gullibility

Blessing the Day

She is the garden she stands beside
She does not know her joy
Little girl lost, uncrowned, dethroned
Wants acceptance but is disowned
Will she survive human-made rules?
It all depends on how she is schooled

In this world where negatives reign
Stay prayed up to avoid its pain
Shine bright star, go deep inside
Do not shun, run or hide
He made you "you" and no one else
Embrace your essence, your song, your self

Realize that life may test you hard
Pray for wisdom, your heart do guard
Keep integrity close, be true
A few will cheer hooray for you

Little girl go be on your way
Loving, believing, and blessing the day.

TM—Last Words

On this birthday I write about TM
His days cut short on a rainy night
One who was innocent; full of fright!

"You got me," were his last words
"Not guilty," the verdict absurd
What was that we just heard?
Not second citizens, a law that says third

Meanwhile, the scene plays again
Reminds us of a time back when
Similar hypocrites devised a plan
Used their laws, killed an innocent man
No death or life is ever in vain
He died for sinners and rose again

"You got me," speaks truth to us
Never settle, but raise a fuss
Many have eyes that just don't see
Need an example like Wonder Stevie
Takes his passion always to the rim
MLK would be proud of him

God's got you now, TM
We carry on our fight with "them"
Those who craft laws and cause a child's
demise
These are the people we doubt and despise
"We got you, TM". We will not forget
Your last words your fatal sunset

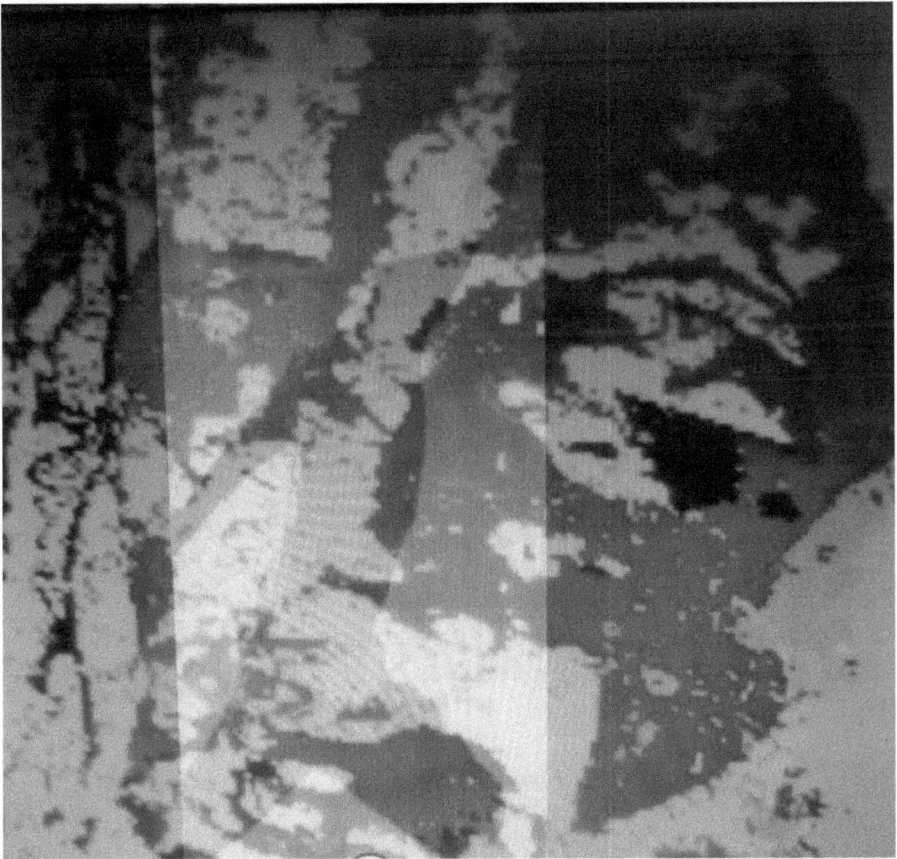

Feelings Don't Come First

Sometimes feelings are not useful; they tangle
what you say
You hold tight, lose control, or push them
quickly away
Rising up or falling down
Voice gets loud or not a sound
Feelings don't come first
They tug on you or worse
If too emotional—they burst

Gender may be an offender
Women, hear this cry
Such and such upsets us
The urge to nag deny
Perhaps, a change of scenery
A walk, warm water or greenery
Will that do the trick, or are feelings too
heavy, too thick?

You are not your feelings; thoughts don't
dominate
Just you pick up your Bible
Read the word and wait
"Be of good cheer!" It says. What's the
meaning of that?
This body temple bears fruit
Self-control it lacks
But strive for perfection; keep feelings at
bay
Seek your peace of spirit; Let feelings drift
away.

A Prodigal More or Less

Not trying to be something that I am not
to prove to others I have got
What they think it takes
Honey, make no mistakes

Some will lift you up while others tear you
down
You are not alone if you wear their crown
Thinking you are something! Yeah! All of that
Sets the stage for a huge blow
Down you fall
Off their wall you go
Get out of there!

You had these friends or so you thought
Family offends and you are caught
God knows where wondering if
anyone cares about you

Men's eyes give more or less
Their measurements are not a test
for you to base your life upon

You are a prodigal
Come on home
For you we write this prodigal poem
Be who you are your essence inside
Let Jesus lead you; let Him guide
You well along the way

How to Love a Friend

Make her think you have the greatest love
Point her towards things above
Where Jesus comes from
Extend your hand
Let your feet, meet hers

When she has to go
Somewhere
Be camouflage
Support and defend
Explain when she cannot comprehend things
Show love in action
Say, "I love you, friend!"

Please, if you may
Never delay or defer
She needs to know
You will be there to care for her

When her day is dark, or hazardous to her
health
Tell her tenderly that life takes time
Be a great believer
Let your light shine

Lift her up
You are a friend
Encourage her heart
Create a win-win
If she doesn't know, go slow
Be like medicine
Make laughter grow in her soul

Your presence is celebratory
like the 4th of July

The world is better since you came along
Bringing her confidence that she belongs
Right where you are

His Grace is What I Know

No amount of asking, looking, lasting,
scrutinizing me
Can change the way I live, or how I choose to
be
Turn the pages; read the books; question high
or low
God has made me who I am; His grace is what I
know

If in your search you find a flaw to feast
your eyes upon
Cast your stone while I repent; submit to the
Holy One

I will not turn, would rather burn like Daniel
in the lions' den
Christ is the way, as in Daniel's day, my
destiny to win
In this life tribulation will come, but I am
of good cheer
No flaring trace will I embrace—victory in Him
is here

To help me through whatever you do; protection
is all around
There is no other able to cover a child when
she is downed
Quiet like night I stand upright; He makes His
grace profound

A ROCK AND A HARD PLACE

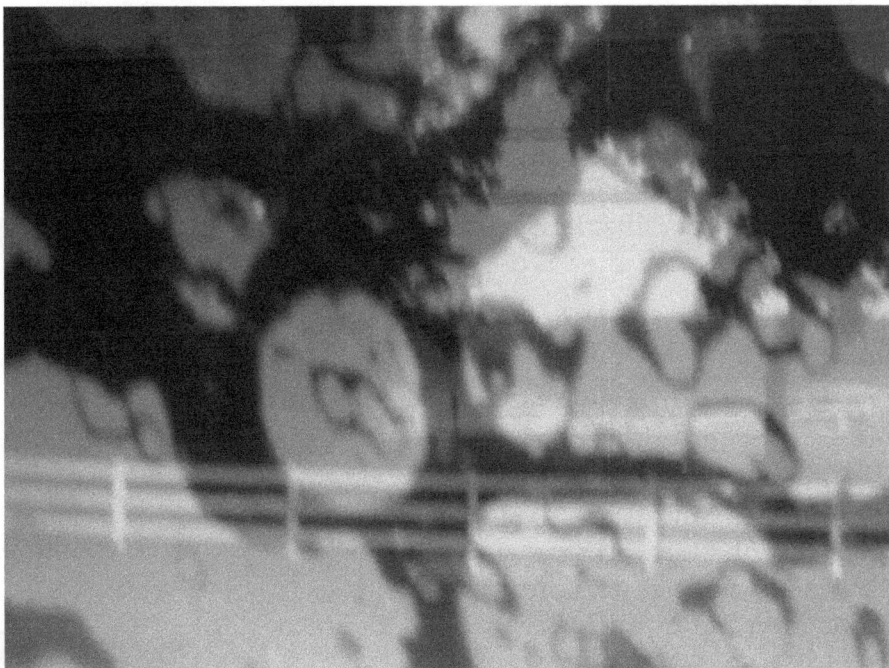

When It Hurts to Smile

When it hurts to smile
Keep smiling still
The world never knows
The strength of the will

When it hurts to love
Let love endure
Nothing is hopeless
Though you are unsure

When it hurts to laugh
This medicine is good
Wallow in a chuckle
Act as if you should

When it hurts to stand alone
Stand--you must do
This is a difficult road
Reserved for the courageous few

When it hurts to hurt
In your heart there is pain
Tears come as friends
Take comfort and know God reigns

When it hurts to live life
Choose life and live
You are a special creature
Honor what God gives

I say this just because
I should have died long ago
If not for His mercy
His grace I'd never know

You Always Remember Me

You always remember me when I am out in space
Faith has vanished somewhere like an item that
is misplaced

You always remember me when I am deep and dark
Look up, I see you smiling, joyful as a lark

You always remember me when others pick me
small
Refuse to give up props like rain they let me
fall

You always remember me. Courage comes or a
friend
To hold my hand or comfort until all chaos
ends

You always remember me. My heart pours with
tears
Your goodness cannot be tallied, a companion
through the years

You always remember me. My lips and heart sing
praise
Like that thief upon the cross, all eyes on
You, we gaze.

How to Beat Up a Friend

Ignore him
Act like he doesn't exist at all
Don't pick up the phone or call
See and don't see
Forget to remember that he was once your boy

Deny envy
Lie--that's how to be
Refrain from being there
Pretend that you care
Stay far away
Have very little to say

Be foggy about how you were
Back in the day
Play with his emotions
Beat him up in bite-sized pieces
Take yourself away
Let falsity rule

Frown a lot. Be cruel
Go on and on live in negativity
Wish all harm comes
So he is like an enemy

Who are you? Do you know?
GET LOST in the One who can show
You how to love again

That Place Called Home

You acted like I wasn't there
Walked past me—did you care?
Now, I know you miss me

Your sure thing is nowhere
Left you with this absentee affair
Going on in your head

Gave you all I could; my allegiance, heart,
and hand,
Loved you, followed your demands
Like a soldier true

Since you were unappreciative
I had to move on,
Your vibe felt weird like I didn't belong

I heard your cronies linger still
Same old game only whispers
of another name, unashamed

Those words, ways, deeds
Misuse of others to succeed
One day tricks will tick in your face

It doesn't matter
I am gone
In search of that place called home

Sometimes

Sometimes
You get tired; and think there is no hope
Sometimes
You feel weary from walking a slippery slope
Sometimes
You are weak, legs collapse and fall
You may be especially broken
From giving others your all

The road sometimes is hard
Tension stands ahead
Those negative thoughts like fire
Quickly sneak in then spread
Far away you spiral; nothing makes any sense
To deeper depths you travel
To bluer blahs more dense

Sometimes
It is these times
When lost or feeling low
Leap into the arms of Jesus
He is where you can go

Someone Cares for You

If you have lost your way, there is still hope
You're not too far astray; reach for help to
cope
Someone cares for you!

I know that life is hard; if you think there
is no way
Toss that suicidal card; just keep yourself in
play
Someone cares for you!

Yes! Someone cares for you! Maybe you don't
see
This God who truly loves folks like you and me

Can we spend some time settling this in your
head?
Don't believe the lies; let truth intervene
instead
What is truth you ask?
A question posed long ago
Jesus Christ said, "Come!"
And off with Him we go
First, you must discard all heavy cargo
You carry in your heart
Speak what's on your mind
Let yourself give way
To His peaceful divine
Presence

Someone cares for you
The King extends His hand
With words pure as truth
He will help you stand

Wounded-hearted Warriors

Take it to the Lord
Tell Him how you feel
Open up you heart
Speak to Him for real

God will listen closely
He sets the record straight
Don't wallow in madness
He will not hesitate
To deal with every mouth
That scandalized your name
Justice will be served
For righteous ones defamed

Wounded-hearted warriors
Must take some time to pray
Are you broken-hearted?
Go without delay

Just remember praise
Is what you need to do
Before deliverance comes
Say to Him, "Thank You"!

Your Heart Is In His Hands

He carries a lot on his shoulders
They are humongous like boulders
Spreading wide across a large wing span
He is often called
A gentle man
Man who comes and goes busily
While you diminish easily into the mass crush
Of swirling things

What good are eyes if they cannot see?
What lurks in the heart of secrecy?

Say something you said in that last text
Talk through the strife that is so complex
Instead of fading like a forgotten act
What you feel may not be fact

You are a lover
Of the Beloved
Take your pleasure in things above
The Strong Man is dazzling, a sheer delight
He serenades sweetly through rough nights
Your heart is in His hands

Your heart is in His hands

Joy to Come

Joy to come, joy to come
I'm looking at Jesus with joy to come
Joy to come, joy to come
I'm trusting in the Savior with joy to come

You may have problems and burdens to bear
Just take them Jesus and leave them there

Trouble won't make me; it sure can't break me
Trust in Jesus with joy to come

Joy to come, Oh, joy to come
I'm looking at Jesus with joy to come

Joy to come, my Lord, joy to come
I'm trusting in the Savior with joy to come

You can kill this body, but not this soul
I will leave this world; my Savior behold

Trouble won't make me, it sure can't break me
I'm trusting in Jesus with joy to come

Joy to come, Oh, joy to come
I'm looking at Jesus with joy to come
Joy to come, my Lord, joy to come
I'm trusting in the Savior with joy to come

Stop!

You need to stop, think about what God has
done for you
Life, health, strength; a place to lay your
head
Money in your pocket to eat your daily bread

You need to stop, thank Him who watches over
you
The omniscient creator who gives His excellent
cue
On how to live this life fresh like morning
dew

You need to stop, tell somebody about His
loving ways
Maybe they would recognize that He deserves
their praise
God who we worship, cherish and adore
Is our great provider, His goodness we dare
not ignore

GOT FAITH

Where Faith Lives

Bombardment--all the time
How do we relax, unwind
It's crazy as hell
We want out
What's this harassment all about?
Anyway!
Perfect peace
That serves our need
Go to the Peacemaker
He will feed
Our hungry soul
Our hungry soul
Our hungry soul
Stand in the house where faith lives
"Now faith is…things hoped for…"
We are not perfect, don't have to be
The Peacemaker is perfect
Rest and see that
Faith in Him is enough!

Say What He Said

I say what He said; not what I see
God's word is truth
Faith lives in me

Say what He said; thoughts, words, habits form
A character that is righteous
A life of faith becomes the norm

Health, finance, relationships, career
His words trust intently
Faith brings them here

Agree with heaven; it comes down to earth
Faith comes by hearing
Watch your seed give birth

Say what He said; walk boldly without fear
We are His beloved
No need to switch gear

Not This Time

I am writing about it
Will smear it in your face
No weapon formed against me; attacks have no
place
This realm where I live is all about faith
Prayer is the answer; God remains true
Let every man be a liar
I am going through
Heated tongues of fire will never undo
This belief I have--not this time!

Crawl back to that space
Your words are like trash
Take them elsewhere before you are bashed
With praise to the God who sits holy on high
He is a way maker, and always nearby
His love is everlasting

The first and last
Strong Man standing
He holds the future, and the past
Firmly in His Hand

My Father, I adore
Still blessing others
Now
Like before!

Got to Keep It Moving

Don't say anything that does not apply
We can be more than we see with the eye

When one door closes; stay steady ahead
There is always another for that one instead

Looking back is no way to win
Got to keep it moving especially when

Time dies daily like times long ago
All things new, the old, let go

You Got to Go

You got to go
You got to go
You got to go through God to get to me
You got to go
You got to go
You got to go through God to get to me

My faith looks up to the one most high
None of his children will the Father deny

You got to go
You got to go
You got to go through God to get to me

The Almighty one of infinity
Your arms too short to reach his chin, you see

You got to go
You got to go
You got to go through God to get to me

Read the Bible book of Exodus
Those Egyptians' they failed to get next to us
All Pharaoh's plans went down the drain
When the sea caved into a cascade of rain

You got to go
You got to go
You got to go through God to get to me

God walks ahead instead of me
Like a pillar of fire at the Red Sea
Blessed going out and coming in
Victory is mine because you can't win

You got to go
You got to go
You got to go through God to get to me

Struck Some Gold

Don't die in misery. Read the word
Haven't you heard? It sustains. It sustains
Away with depression, strongholds must go
Toss all negatives out the window.
In your soul
Feel the love of God!

Struck some gold in the word of God
While reading there emerged a glow
Joy dispersed letting me know
It is within reach.
His promises live
All are true
All especially written for me and you

We don't have to look like it
Just got to be
Children of Abraham
Have faith—see
We like Christ share the same
Blessing of God in His name
Receive! Receive! Receive and give
True abundance Christ died, so live!

Come! Eat! Every word is good
It is like Psalms. It is like Psalms.

AND LOVE

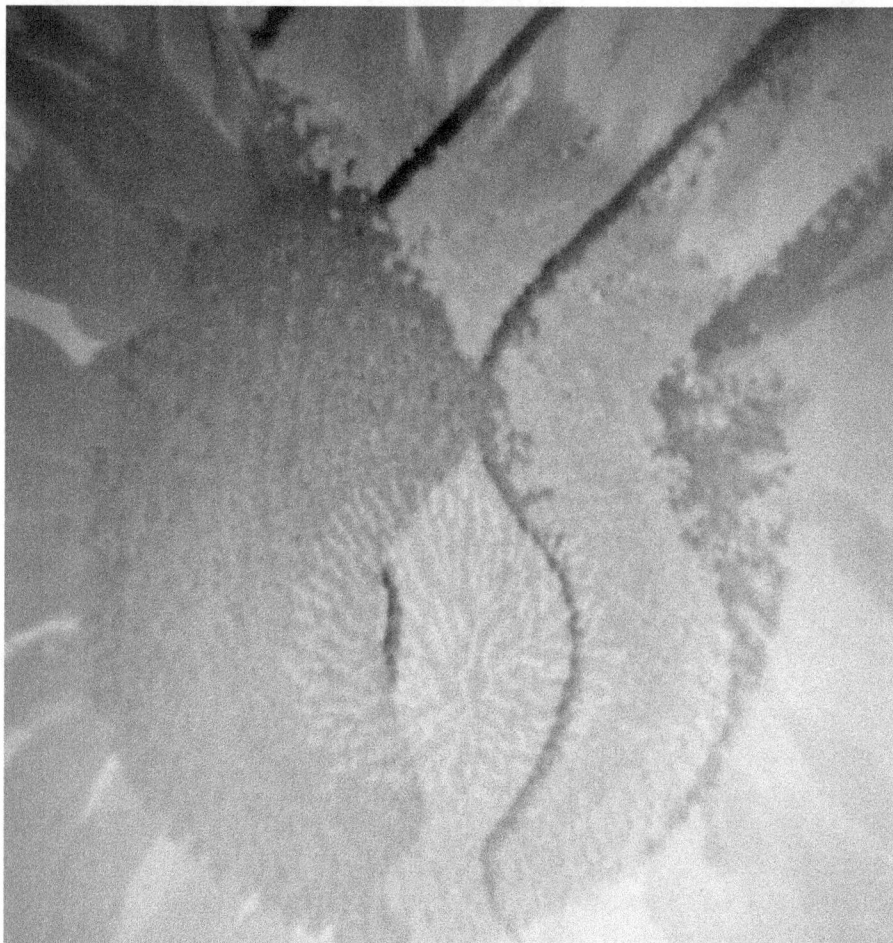

Out on a Limb

I missed my mother when she died
Didn't know what I would do
God held me strong each day that passed
I looked to Him anew

God is love! That never got through
Before death's passing lane
Time did heal; I could feel
His presence was truly insane

The very main one is His son
I long for, and enjoy
A beautiful meadow cannot compare
He brings such peace and joy

In quiet times, heart hungry, alone
I kneel in search of Him
Like Zacchaeus climbed that tree
Excited, out on a limb

It was He who first sought me
This King did not hesitate
I am drawn to amazing love
Though He did initiate

Family Drama

You haven't gone to see your mother
In place of her you substitute another
Words from your mouth you delay
You refuse to forgive or say, "I apologize!"
Like a steamship you prod along
Thinking you are right; knowing she is wrong
Family support you subdue
Who will you run to; to whom will you cry
Your role you easily deny

Throughout life we make mistakes
We never mend the wounds
But when our loved one is gone
They always leave too soon
Our selfishness we placate
We do not let love heal hate

God is here to care for you
Cast all negatives to Him from you
Leave an opening to be changed
Confront your temptation to live estranged

Family dramas and crazy mamas
Sons, daughters, all the rest
God specializes
He is best at healing broken-hearts.

When You Come Back to Me

When you come back to me
I will be still in love
Still in love with you

When you have a change of heart
We can start over again
Let's do it again
Because I will be still in love
Still in love with you

Love is kind; it's genuine
Love is not fickle, like a player's lines
You are the one I set my eyes on
I am the one you desire

When you come back to me
I will be still in love
Still in love with you

Following Destiny

He did it all for me
It took some time to see
Thought I was following destiny

Some people they followed Him
I did not go with them
Liked living life on a whim

He saw what I would do
Forget the childhood I knew
In search of thrills brand new

There on the other side
I was pumped and full of pride
But a pain was throbbing inside

One day a lyrical song
Made me feel the joy I longed
His presence was where I belonged

He revealed His love for me
It took some time to see
Jesus Christ was my destiny

Jesus Christ was my destiny
Jesus Christ, my destiny

Just Do It

Women hear me, understand
He says things aren't going too well with his
wife.
He wishes it was you he fell
In love with

Says he wants you instead of her
But what about his children or the history
He created in the past? Will you let it be
See and don't see that's what you say
Oh, I got it! You want a play
His lady you will be, in spite everything on
display
I shake my head, just give it some time
Allow the game to go, until it unwinds
No! No! No!

Listen, girl! I'm talking to you
What makes you think he and his wife are
through?
Go about your business; just get lost
How can he be a family man with you in the
sauce?
Looking lovely with your devilish self
It's not about you, go somewhere else
God won't bless mess especially when
You are spreading your love like real thin
Living the chaos in his world
You are better than that,
Hear me, girl!

Don't be the one committing sin
Sin, yeah, I said it because that's what it is
His relationship trouble is none of your biz
You won't ever get God's promises by sinning

He laid out your blessings from the beginning
The one He has is especially made
To match who you are, so don't make a bad
trade
You will lose out, those blessings sent
elsewhere
Choose to be strong, have courage to bear
Temptation always has a dead end
If you walk that path, you will descend

Wait on the Lord. He can bring you through it
Walk! Leave that married man alone
Just do it!
Hang up the phone!

Benefits

I think there are benefits to looking in the heart
Truth is one of them; a good place to start
Those issues that dwell there do tell where I'm at
Sometimes hard to face; I'd rather be a distract
But when I go there; I come around again
A distract often falls wallowing in her sin

Back to those benefits—the Lord is truly good
I wish to be consistent and do things as I should
Discipline may help; so would a prayer
God who is relentless can surely take me there
He is the ultimate cheer leader, rooting everyday
"Forget not His benefits"
He tells me this I say!

Love is Going Crazy

There is no beginning
There is no end
Without You in my life
I would never comprehend
Your purpose or your plan
Responsibility You demand
From the meek and lowly
A call to be holy, holy, holy

Just like You
To have, to hold what is true
I give myself away
As Jesus did, I do

I am privileged
Walking hand in hand
With the great Creator
Doing what He commands

Strapped to His word
Old feelings reappear
My love is going crazy
Dancing to what I hear

No one can ever break us
No storm ever subdue
The bond we share is solid
Loveliest first love we ever knew

No Lack of Love in Him

Healing power gone out from Him
A woman reached to touch His hem
Glorious virtue, the glorified One
She searched the world, and found none
Like Him
Crowds pushed; they shoved; she craved
Desperately, she reached
They gave… her a piece of their mind
Never mind what others say
When opportunity comes your way
Reach out for Him
His love can save
You go ahead, misbehave
A blessing waits for you
Glorious virtue the glorified One
He restores; the work was done

"Who touched my clothes?"

Jesus looked around to see
Who He had known the woman to be

"It was me! I stand accused
For so many years this body abused
By sickness none could explain
I heard you were coming
Could not refrain myself
I had to touch you,
Oh, virtuous One!"

Her fear came after the healing was done
And my Lord passionately said,
"Relax yourself! Your faith is intact.
Go in peace."
There is no lack of love in Him.

Charity

You are like a shining star
Haloing bright in the sky so far
I look up. You see me
Luminous body glory be
Walking earth streaking down
Lifted hands when You come around
Meek and lowly the first and last
At closer view grandeur vast

Living water from mountain peaks
Pure as nature parables speak
Words richly laden with truth
Come to us renew our youth
We follow You! Your path, Your way
Bread of Life we surrender today
A change of heart is due right now
At Your name every knee shall bow

Light light shining bright
Coming from the left coming from the right
Reveal Yourself, revelation Star
Many do not know how precious You are
I hope this poem helps them see
You are all heart, charity

Now and Forever

Fired Up

Will you be fired up about being on a team?
Excited, mad crazy
You know what I mean!
Scream! Yell!
Vocal cords display
Not spending time in hell
Won't live eternity that way

Call us weird or out of touch
What Jesus did was not too much
Committed is how He stood
Bold eye to eye
Focused on what's good, and God glorify!
Fired up to the very end
A perfect model for us to ascend to.

Dreams

Imagination takes me where
I never been
Or would not dare
Go

Dreams

Reminders of places been
People met now and then
Experiences to come
And some gone

Dreams

Familiar invaders of the night

See mom's face, "Are you alright"?
Comfort knowing she's still here
Ride her wave a smile and cheer

Dreams

Dwell so well in my abode
Here am I
The invited guest
Off tonight on another quest

Dreams

While I sleep content matters
Weird nightmares how they splatter
Fearful me to pitter patters
A terrible load explodes

Dreams

Thrust themselves into daylight
Speak to others about my plight
But not so fresh as vivid night

Dreams

Don't remember some at all
I search for them cannot recall
One foggy episode

Dreams

Come inside deep-seated rest
Another world to curse or bless
Come they may be to test
A brand new day

Habitations

My life is your life; your life is mine
Eternally driven
Placed here by design

There is no difference between you and me
All live, exist
In the Holy of Holies

Do you love Him? Does your life show signs?
His promises are not for those
Who run only in times—of danger

God preserves those who abide totally in Him
No emotional living
Fluctuations or whims

In the shadow of the Almighty; there is
contemplation
Is that where you live?
Is He your habitation?

A Holy Nazarene

So much on the outside tries to get in
How does one manage or even defend
Unquenchable desires answer when they call
Abandon senses, morality and all

What is submission, doing what you do?
How much is too much; will you ever be
through?
Running like a chicken, hiding from light
Stretching yourself thin with a budget gone
tight

When did this happen? Were you pulled away?
Your head, swelling high on many a day
God took you to a place, but you could not see
How word works wonders for you and me

No need to fight battles parading in your
heart
Invite the ultimate Counselor to stop them
where they start
His speech is peaceful. He is serene
A faithful redeemer, a Holy Nazarene

Jesus Christ, the Holy One

What I have is what I need
Out of turmoil comes a seed
Without thorns, I can't grow
What's in me, He will show

Je-sus Christ, the Holy One
I am heir with the Son
Je-sus Christ, the Holy One
I am heir with the Son

I won't hold back, I won't hold back
Let me give
I won't hold back, I won't hold back
Let me live for
Je-sus Christ, the Holy One
I am heir with the Son

Thank You Lord, for heavy loads
Lead me down the stony roads
You won't put more on me
than I can bear
I come to You, cast all my care

I won't hold back, I won't hold back
Let me give
I won't hold back, I won't hold back
Let me live for
Je-sus Christ, the Holy One
I am heir with the Son
Je-sus Christ the Holy One
I am heir with the Son

Forever

I will tell you about forever; the little that
I know
Forever is this place where the good will
grow.
Does that bring you joy; it certainly does to
me
Father, make it happen ever so quickly; change
us forever instantly

Day will be extended; night will be no more
The mind can't comprehend it; will I meet you
on that shore?
Forever is very beautiful, a city made of gold
A sweet bye and bye, an awesome sight to
behold

In the days of my youth, this is what I was
told
It remains the gospel truth; now that I am old
Old makes me happy; I'm marching forward to
A fellowship and worship, a body sparkling new

Age will never wander in or around any face
Jesus went long ago to prepare for us a place
The fairest of ten thousand, our bright and
morning star
This journey to forever will take us just that
far

In the twinkling of an eye; we follow right
away
Where memory catches fire on that happy day
Onward to forever being present and near
Walk by faith in spirit; what is there to
fear?

He loves us so much; He gave His only son
Our Father who is in heaven is the cherished
one

Forever

ACKNOWLEDGEMENTS

Thank you, Father God for inspiring me to
write your words through the power of your
son, Jesus Christ, and the creative
power of the Holy Spirit.

Special thanks to all of you who encouraged me
in writing this second book of poems. Your
words did not fall on deaf ears.

I am always appreciative of my loving husband
who makes me smile and listens to my poems. He
is a great supporter and friend.

Finally, thanks to those who have read,
recited, and shared my poems with others,
especially young people who will always
hold a special place in my heart, a flashback
to my days of teaching.

We found in Him a resting place, and He has
made us glad!

About The Author

SE Scott was born in Summerton, South Carolina. She has lived in Florida, New York, and New Jersey.
She now resides in Columbia, South Carolina with her husband, Lynn.
Since retiring as a teacher of English for 30 years, SE has devoted much of her time to writing, media production, community activities, travel, and family.
She also lectures about writing and poetry in schools and other institutions around the country.
SE Scott is co-author of the play, A Pearl of a Girl, a coming of age story about five teenage girls.
This is SE Scott's second published work. Her first book of poems, Keep Smiling, Standing Strong is available on Amazon.com and other book stores. Some of her poems can be viewed on YouTube under the name Mustang2lady. You can email SE at essiece@gmail.com, and listen to her talk show, Here By DeSign on Blogtalkradio.com.

* * *